DIGGERS

Andrew Langley

W
FRANKLIN WATTS
LONDON•SYDNEY

 An Appleseed Editions book

First published in 2010 by Franklin Watts
338 Euston Road, London NW1 3BH

Franklin Watts Australia
Hachette Children's Books
Level 17/207 Kent St, Sydney, NSW 2000

© 2010 Appleseed Editions

Created by Appleseed Editions Ltd,
Well House, Friars Hill, Guestling,
East Sussex TN35 4ET

Planning and production by Discovery Books Limited
Designed by D.R. ink
Cover design by Blink Media
Edited by James Nixon

ISBN: 978 1 4451 0027 2

Dewey Classification: 629.2'25

A CIP catalogue for this book is available from the British Library.

Photograph acknowledgements
Alamy Images: pp. 12 (Greenshoots Communications), 13 bottom (William Caram), 14 (www.white-windmill.
co.uk), 20 bottom (Justin Kase zfivez), 23 top (David Burton), 23 bottom (Paul Springett), 27 bottom (David R.
Frazier/Photolibrary); Getty Images: p. 26 (David McNew); Istockphoto.com: pp. 15 top (Robert Kyllo), 15 bottom
(Don Bayley), 17 bottom (Maciej Korzekwa); J C Bamford Excavators Ltd: pp. 5 top, 10, 11 bottom; QinetiQ:
p. 29; Shutterstock: 5 bottom (Marilyn Barbone), 9 top (Stanislav Komogorov), 11 top, 13 top, 16, 17 top (Tom
Oliveira), 18, 19 bottom (Mark Atkins), 20 top (Robert Asento), 21 top, 21 bottom (Michael Zysman), 22 (Dmitri
Melnik), 27 top; Siemens Industry Solutions: p. 25 bottom; Terex Corporation: p. 9 bottom; Volvo CE: pp. 4, 6, 7,
8, 19 top, 28.

Cover photos: J C Bamford Excavators Ltd: top; Istockphoto.com: bottom.

Printed in China

Franklin Watts is a division of Hachette Children's Books,
www.hachette.co.uk

Contents

What is a digger?

A digger is a powerful machine that moves earth and rock. It is used for all kinds of building work, from laying roads to digging tunnels.

There are many types of digger. Some dig **trenches**, or drill holes in the ground. Others are used to knock down buildings or clear away rocks and **rubble**.

Big, strong tyres, with ridges, grip slippery or rough ground.

Cab: where the driver sits

Boom: main part of the arm

Dipper arm: second part of the arm

Loader: scoops up material from the ground

Bucket: digs into the earth

Rams: moving rods that change the angle of the arm or bucket

Mini-digger

Most diggers are big, but a mini-digger is very small. It could easily fit in an big digger's loader. Mini-diggers are used for work in very tight spaces.

Crawler tracks: for travel on muddy ground

In the cab

The driver sits in the cab. There are glass screens around it which give the driver a good view on all sides. The glass also keeps out dust and rain.

Cab comforts

Modern cabs have heated seats to keep the drivers warm in winter. Some have **air conditioning** to keep them cool in summer, too.

The driver works levers and pedals in the cab. Each one controls a different part of the digger.

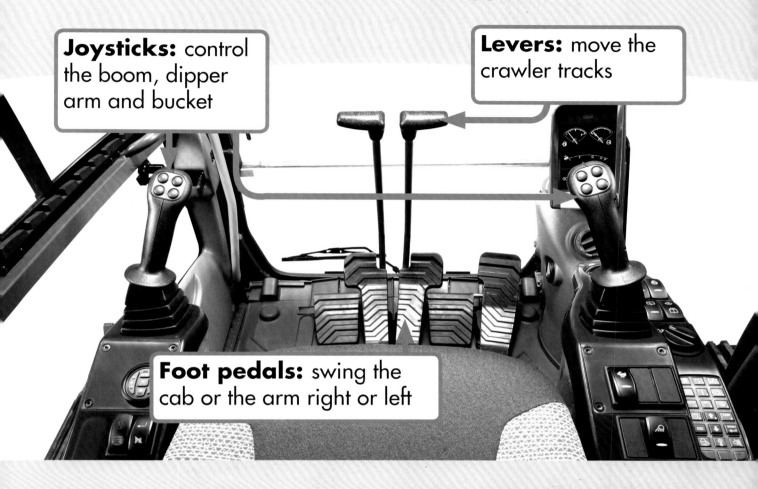

Joysticks: control the boom, dipper arm and bucket

Levers: move the crawler tracks

Foot pedals: swing the cab or the arm right or left

Engine

A digger needs a lot of power. The **diesel** engine moves the arms and bucket, as well as the wheels or tracks.

Engine

Excavators

An **excavator** is the most useful kind of machine on a building site. It can dig trenches, lift heavy objects and carry earth in its big bucket.

Cab

The excavator cab is set on a platform above the crawler tracks. It can turn in a complete circle, moving material from one side to the other.

Hydraulic rams

The arms and buckets of a digger are moved by **rams**. These are fitted inside cylinders. When a liquid, such as oil, is forced into the cylinder, the ram moves up or down. This is called **hydraulic** power.

Cylinder

Ram

Giant digger

The **RH400** is the biggest hydraulic excavator ever built. It weighs over **1070** tonnes. Its bucket can lift **94** tonnes. This is enough to fill the biggest truck in just five scoops!

Backhoe loaders

The digger you are most likely to see is a backhoe loader. It has digging tools at each end.

On the back is a long movable arm with a small bucket. This is the **backhoe**. On the front is a big bucket for picking up rubble. This is the loader. The cab seat swivels right around so the driver can operate either.

Loader

Backhoe

Arm

The arm connects the cab with the backhoe. It has two parts – the **boom** and the **dipper arm**. Together, these can stretch a long way up or down.

Backhoe tools

Special tools can be fitted to the backhoe in place of the bucket. These include a drill and a hammer for breaking concrete.

Dredgers

A dredger is used to dig up **silt** and mud from the bottom of rivers or the sea. This is done to make the water deeper so that boats can pass through.

Some dredgers are like a big excavator mounted on a boat. This has a backhoe for scooping out the mud and loading it on to a barge.

Bucket

The bucket on a digger has sharp metal teeth, which tear through the earth. Some buckets open and shut so they can grab the soil.

Suction dredger

Another kind of dredger uses the power of suction. It sucks up mud and other materials through a long tube, just like a vacuum cleaner. The suction dredgers on the *Queen of the Netherlands* ship (below) have been used to recover bits of crashed aircraft.

Pile drivers

A **pile** driver is a machine that hammers strong rods deep into the earth. These rods are called piles. They make a firm **foundation** for buildings on soft ground.

An excavator lifts a heavy weight and places it on the pile (below). A diesel engine then powers the weight to **vibrate** up and down. This drives the pile downwards into the ground.

Weight

Pile

Crane

The pile driver is sometimes attached to a crane. This lifts up the weight on the end of a cable.

Demolition

Diggers can be used for destroying buildings, too. Excavators knock down a building by ramming the walls with its arm. A rock breaker attached to the arm (right) breaks through the steel or concrete.

Bulldozers

A building site has to be flattened and cleared of rubble. This is usually the job of the bulldozer.

A bulldozer is a powerful machine with a large metal blade on the front. This pushes the stones and other rubble into heaps. These can then be loaded on to trucks and taken away.

Blade

Crawler tracks

Instead of wheels, most bulldozers move on a pair of tracks. These are wide belts, with ridges that help the machine grip the muddy ground.

Snow plough

A snow plough is a kind of bulldozer. It uses its blade to push snow off roads.

This snow plough (right) has been fitted with a snow blower. The snow is cut up and blown out by a fan turning at high speed.

Snow blower

Scraping and paving

Before a road is built, the ground has to be made level and smooth. A scraper is a machine with metal blades, which slice off the top layer of the ground.

Scraper

After the scraper comes the paving machine. The paving machine moves slowly along the road, spreading a thin layer of **asphalt**. Asphalt is a mixture of hot tar and gravel.

Paving machine

Double engine

Some huge scrapers have two engines. One drives the front wheels, and the other drives the back wheels.

Rollers

The roller drives along behind the paver. It squeezes down the hot asphalt and leaves it smooth and hard.

The lightest rollers (left) are operated by someone walking behind. The heaviest ones have two large drums and can weigh more than 20 tonnes.

Many diggers will be operated by **remote control**.
The driver will not sit in the cab, but at a control
centre nearby.

This remote-controlled
digger is used by the
army. It saves soldiers
from having to drive
into danger zones.

Glossary

air conditioning a system for controlling the temperature of the air

asphalt a mixture of tar and crushed gravel or sand

backhoe a movable arm for digging

boom the first part of a digger's arm

bore make a hole in something with a tool, such as a drill

diesel an engine fuel made from petroleum

dipper arm the second part of a digger's arm, with the bucket on the end

drill bit the cutting part at the tip of the drill

excavator a powerful digging machine

foundation the lowest level of a building, built below the ground

fuel cell a power system which uses hydrogen instead of a fossil fuel, such as coal or oil

hydraulic power that comes from pushing liquid through a tube

hydrogen a colourless gas, used as a fuel to create electrical power

joystick a hand-control lever

landfill site a huge hole in the ground where rubbish is dumped

loader the arms and bucket at the front of a digger for lifting and carrying things

mine a place where coal or other minerals are dug out of the ground

pile a strong beam driven into the ground as foundation for a building

pollution damage to the air, land or water with dirty and poisonous substances

ram a rod which drives the working parts of a digger

remote control controlling something from a distant point

rubble pieces of rock, mud and other waste material

silt a muddy mixture of sand, clay and other fine minerals found on the river or sea bed

trench a long, narrow ditch

vibrate shake up and down very quickly

Index

Websites

www.jcbexplore.com
This website about diggers is packed with fun games and activities.

www.kenkenkikki.jp/special/e_index.html
Learn how digging machines work.

www.pbs.org/wgbh/buildingbig/tunnel/challenge/
Take the 'Tunnel Challenge' and find out about tunnel building.